ISLAND HERITAGE™
PUBLISHING
A DIVISION OF THE MADDEN CORPORATION

94-411 Kō'aki Street
Waipahu, Hawai'i 96797-2806
Orders: (800) 468-2800
Information: (808) 564-8800
Fax: (808) 564-8877
islandheritage.com

ISBN: 1-61710-173-7
First Edition, Second Printing—2013
COP 130207

Tūtū Nēnē The Hawaiian Mother Goose Rhymes

Written by **Debra Ryll** • Illustrated by **Stephanie Britt**

ISLAND HERITAGE™
PUBLISHING

Old Tūtū Nēnē
When she wanted to wander,
Would soar on the tradewinds,
From Niʻihau to Kauaʻi, Oʻahu, Molokaʻi,
Lānaʻi, Maui, Kahoʻolawe, and (whew!)
the Big Island over yonder.

- Tūtū. Grandmother
- Nēnē. A rare, protected Hawaiian goose

Little Miss Aku sat on a pōhaku,

Swatting mosquitoes all day.

Along came a spider,

Who sat down beside her

And scared the buggahs away.

- **Pōhaku.** Rock
- **Buggah.** Pidgin English for bug

This little menehune went to the lūʻau,
This little menehune stayed home.
This little menehune ate kālua pig,
This little menehune had none.
And this little menehune cried, "Auwē! Auwē!"
All the way home.

- Menehune. Hawaiian elf
- Kālua pig. Pork baked in an imu
- Lūʻau. Hawaiian feast
- Auwē! Oh dear! Alas!

6

Find a pig and roast him,
Wrap him in tī.
Bake him in the imu,
For the cousins and me!

• **Tī.** A woody green plant
• **Imu.** Underground oven

Sticky rice hot,
Sticky rice cold.
Sour poi in the pot,
Nine days old!
Some like it hot,
Some like it cold.
Some like it in the pot,
Nine days old!

• Poi. Pounded taro

8

Fish-cake! Fish-cake!
Rice and Spam.
Make me a plate lunch,
As fast as you can!

- **Fish-cake.** Pressed seafood, used in local dishes
- **Spam.** A favorite Island food
- **Plate lunch.** Hawaiian "fast food"

9

Sumo Takahashi sat on the wall,

Sumo Takahashi had a great fall.

And all King Kalākaua's horses, and all of his men,

Couldn't put Mr. Takahashi up on that wall again.

- **Sumo. A very large wrestler**
- **Kalākaua. A famous Hawaiian king**

The itsy bitsy bufo
Went up the cane shack spout.
Down came the rain
And washed the bufo out.
Up came the lā
And dried up all the rain.
And the itsy bitsy bufo
Went up the spout again.

• **Bufo.** Toad
• **Lā.** Sun

Ua, ua, go away,
Hilo's wet enough today,
And all the tourists want to play!

- Ua. Rain
- Hilo. A rainy town on the Big Island

Pi'ilani picked a peck of pickled poke.

A peck of pickled poke Pi'ilani picked.

If Pi'ilani picked a peck of pickled poke,

Where's the peck of pickled poke Pi'ilani picked?

(Polihale, probably.)

- **Poke. Raw fish dish**
- **Polihale. A beach on the island of Kaua'i.**

14

Little Keola Kehau,
Sings for her kaukau.
What shall she eat?
Sweet bread and laulau.

- **Kaukau.** Food
- **Sweet bread.** Portuguese bread
- **Laulau.** Local dish wrapped in tī leaves

15

Little Kekoa sat in the corner,
Eating his liliko'i pie.
He put in his thumb,
Took out a crumb,
And said, "'Ono ka mea'ai!"

- Liliko'i. Passion fruit
- 'Ono. Delicious
- Mea'ai. Food

Little Kāne Polu, come blow your conch!
The 'ahi's in the ocean, the limu's on the beach.
Where's the little kāne who picks 'opihi on the reef?
Under the coco palm, fast asleep!

- Kāne. Man or boy
- Polu. Blue
- Conch. Seashell used as a horn
- 'Ahi. Tuna
- Limu. Seaweed
- 'Opihi. Limpet

Old Tūtū Pele sang a fierce mele,

And the lava flowed into the sea.

When it got there,

Kalapana was bare,

So Pele made sand for the beach.

- **Tūtū. Grandmother**
- **Pele. Volcano Goddess**
- **Mele. Song or chant**
- **Lava. Volcanic rock**
- **Kalapana. A black sand beach on the Big Island**

18

Malia had a little mo'o,

Its skin was green and yellow.

And everywhere Malia went,

The mo'o was sure to holoholo.

It followed her to school one day,

Which was against the kumu's rule.

It made the keiki laugh and play,

To see a mo'o at school!

- Mo'o. Gecko or lizard
- Holoholo. Go
- Kumu. Teacher
- Keiki. Child

21

Kaleo Kalani,
Haupia and pie,
Kissed the wahine and made them cry.
When the kāne came out to play,
Kaleo Kalani ran away.

- **Haupia.** Coconut pudding
- **Wahine.** Woman or girl
- **Kāne.** Man or boy

Ring around the pua nani,
Pocket full of loke lani.
Ashes, Ashes!
We all fall down.

- Pua. Flower
- Nani. Beautiful
- Loke lani. Small red rose

Little Hoʻokipa has a puka in her net,
And doesn't know how to mend it.
Leave her alone, when the ʻohana
comes home,
With kōkua they'll surely tend it.

- **Puka. Hole**
- **ʻOhana. Family**
- **Kōkua. Help, assistance**

Kimo and Ulu went up the pu'u,

To fetch a lei of maile.

Ulu slid down,

On a tī leaf she found,

And Kimo came tumbling after.

- Pu'u. Hill
- Lei. Garland or necklace
- Maile. A fragrant vine
- Tī. A woody green plant with many uses

25

Twinkle, twinkle little hōkū,
How I wonder all about you.
Up above the 'āina so high,
Like a kaimana in the sky.

- **Hōkū.** Star
- **'Āina.** Land, earth
- **Kaimana.** Diamond

26

There was a wahine,
Who lived in a shoe.
She had so many keiki,
She knew just what to do.
She fed them all poi, instead of bread,
Whispered "Me ke aloha," and sent
them to bed.

- **Wahine. Woman**
- **Keiki. Child**
- **Poi. Pounded taro**
- **Me ke aloha. With love.**

Here is the 'ohana,
Here are the kūpuna.
Open your heart,
And feel the aloha.

- 'Ohana. Family
- Kūpuna. Ancestor
- Aloha. Love

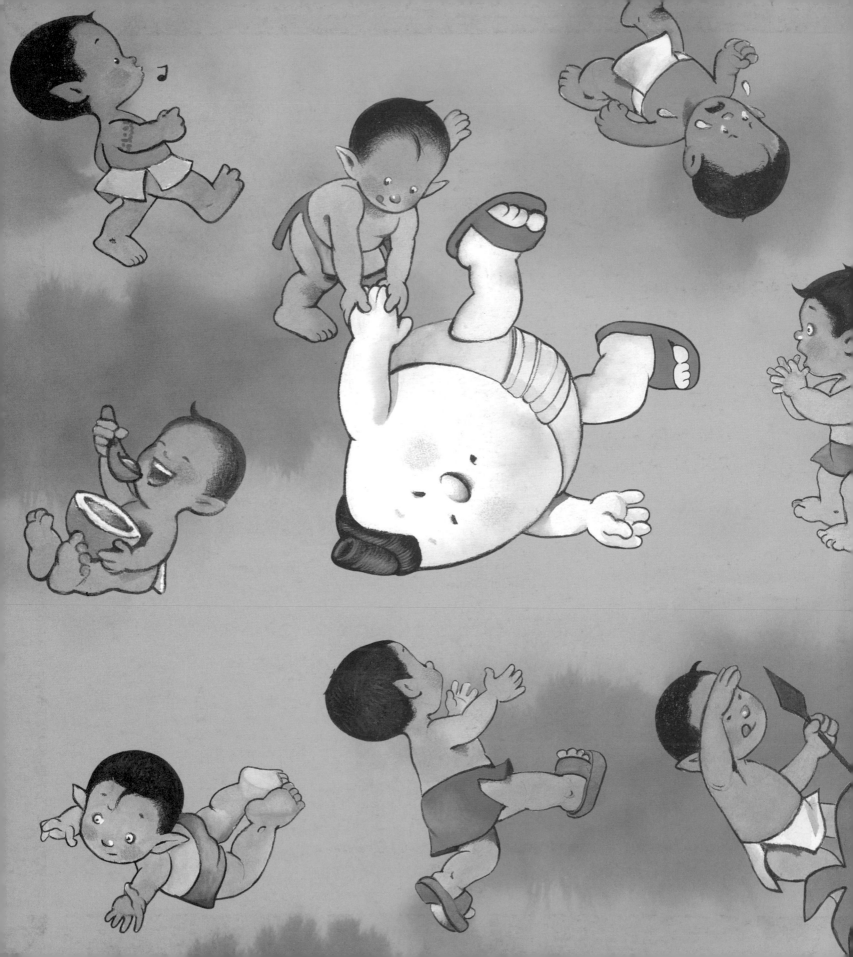